TRUMPET SOUND EFFECTS

**CIRCULAR BREATHING,
SPLIT TONES,
EXTREME EMBOUCHURES,
AND MUCH MORE!**

To access audio visit:
www.halleonard.com/mylibrary

Enter Code
6685-1738-2389-7421

CRAIG PEDERSEN AND UELI DÖRIG

For those with open ears and an open heart

Berklee Press

Editor in Chief: Jonathan Feist
Vice President of Online Learning and Continuing Education: Debbie Cavalier
Assistant Vice President of Operations for Berklee Media: Robert F. Green
Assistant Vice President of Marketing and Recruitment for Berklee Media: Mike King
Dean of Continuing Education: Carin Nuernberg
Editorial Assistants: Reilly Garrett, Emily Jones, Zoë Lustri
Cover Design: Small Mammoth Design
Cover Photo: Ueli Dörig
Hose Trumpet Photo: Ueli Dörig

ISBN 978-0-87639-157-0

1140 Boylston Street
Boston, MA 02215-3693 USA
(617) 747-2146

Visit Berklee Press Online at
www.berkleepress.com

Study with

■ **BERKLEE ONLINE**

online.berklee.edu

DISTRIBUTED BY

HAL•LEONARD®
CORPORATION
7777 W. BLUEMOUND RD. P.O. BOX 13819
MILWAUKEE, WISCONSIN 53213

Visit Hal Leonard Online at
www.halleonard.com

Berklee Press, a publishing activity of Berklee College of Music, is a not-for-profit educational publisher.
Available proceeds from the sales of our products are contributed to the scholarship funds of the college.

CONTENTS

ACKNOWLEDGMENTS

CRAIG PEDERSEN

This book wouldn't be possible without the input of Scott Thomson and Taylor Brook; the open and patient teaching of John McNeil, Laurie Frink, Louis Ranger, and Karen Donnelly; the creative input of Matt Ouimet, Stephen Boudreau, and Jake Von Wurden; and all those who have pushed the boundaries of trumpet playing and music before us. Thank you!

UELI DÖRIG

I'd like to thank my beautiful wife Claudia for keeping me company on my adventurous journeys; Jonathan Feist, our editor at Berklee Press, for the great source of inspiration that his professionalism is to me; and most importantly, I'd like to thank my brother-in-arms Craig Pedersen for being such a wonderful free spirit and friend.

RECORDING CREDITS

These tracks were recorded, mixed, and mastered by Matt Ouimet in Ottawa, Ontario, Canada. They feature Craig Pedersen on trumpet, Stephen Boudreau on piano, Jake Von Wurden on electric bass, and Matt Ouimet on drums.

INTRODUCTION

This book presents twenty-seven extended techniques for the trumpet. While the book is titled "*Trumpet Sound Effects*," we think of them as general tools and techniques to help you realize the music inside of you.

There is a rich history in music and art of extending beyond the conceived limitations of any given instrument. Thus, we have endeavored in this book to treat these extended techniques with the respect and care that we feel they deserve, while providing content for a broad range of musicians. Novice and amateur trumpet players will find the explanations and exercises to be clear and simple, more experienced players will find explanations of many of the extended techniques common in contemporary classical repertoire and jazz, and composers will find a resource of many of the sonic possibilities of the trumpet.

Have fun exploring them, and please be patient with yourself. Some of these techniques require a lot of time to master. If you let it, this book will make you a stronger musician by opening your ears to new possibilities, expanding your trumpet's sonic palette, pushing you out of your comfort zone, and exposing you to new and challenging musical situations.

HOW TO USE THIS BOOK

There are two main sections in this book. Part I will help you to learn the extended techniques, and part II will help you apply them. Always make sure to listen closely to the recorded examples before attempting each technique and etude, and follow instructions to rest where indicated. Learning extended techniques can push your abilities to the limits, and the last thing you want to do is injure yourself.

To access the accompanying audio, go to www.halleonard.com/mylibrary and enter the code found on the first page of this book. This will grant you instant access to every example. Examples that include audio are marked with an audio icon.

HOW TO USE EXTENDED TECHNIQUES

Working on these extended techniques will help you to enhance the knowledge of your body and your instrument. With every technique you learn, you will gain more control. The more control we have, the more freedom we have to express ourselves.

Experimentation is key to finding a personal and musical approach to using extended techniques. Some people prefer to begin with a clear musical concept in mind, while others prefer to begin with technique. Whichever the starting point for you, always seek to learn the other, gaining both musical and technical control. Using extended techniques is like using spices while cooking. If you apply the right amount of spices, the result will taste good. But always remember: too much spice can ruin even the simplest dish. It is one thing to be capable of playing an extended technique and another to use it musically.

NOTATION

When dealing with extended techniques and composition, it's important to note that there are no fully codified systems of extended technique notation. While some of the notation in this book draws on convention, much of it is novel, and we have strived for clarity in notating these techniques. When confronted with a new notation and technique, it's important to take time to consider it thoroughly and to not be afraid to look into the description in the notes of the score, or earlier in the book.

Some of the techniques in this book sound very close to how they are notated. Mouthpiece popping is an example of this. The (x) notehead denotes a nonconventional playing technique, while the placement on the staff indicates resultant pitch.

FIG. I.1. X Noteheads for Pitched Nonconventional Technique

However, some of the other techniques are notated to reflect an action to be taken, and don't reflect the end result sound. A good example of this is singing through the instrument. The top line represents a pitch to be sung, while the bottom, notated with (x) noteheads, represents which fingerings to use. The resultant effect is not a change in pitch, but instead an interruption of the sung pitch.

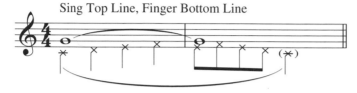

FIG. I.2. X Noteheads for Fingered Technique

Whenever possible, refer to the examples on the companion audio and notes in the score.

PART I

Technique

1. WIND SOUNDS

Alternative Names: wind, unpitched blowing

To produce a wind sound, blow air through the instrument without playing a note. A variety of wind sounds can be produced on the trumpet. While the most basic method is to inhale and exhale through the instrument with a slack embouchure, there are other approaches, each producing slightly different sounds.

First, place your lips over the mouthpiece (Mpc.) while inhaling and exhaling. You can also remove the mouthpiece completely, and place your lips over the mouthpiece receiver, or turn the mouthpiece around so that the cup is against the mouthpiece receiver, and then blow into the mouthpiece shank. You can also blow across the mouthpiece or the mouthpiece receiver, as if you were blowing across an open bottle.

FIG. 1.1. Wind Sounds Notation

Experiment with different strengths and speeds of blowing and sucking air to find different sounds. Try continuously blowing while moving your valves. You will find that pushing down each valve changes the sound of the air. Making wind sounds while continuously moving your valves can create interesting textures.

The great thing about this technique is that you can do it without stopping to breathe. You can play wind sounds continuously by both inhaling and exhaling through the instrument.

Exercises

1. Inhale and exhale through the instrument using a variety of fingering combinations. Pitches on the staff below indicate valve positions.

FIG. 1.2. Wind Sounds Exercise 1

2. Inhale and exhale through the instrument while rapidly moving your valves.

FIG. 1.3. Wind Sounds Exercise 2

2. SINGING THROUGH THE INSTRUMENT

Instead of buzzing your lips through the trumpet, you can sing through it. This causes your voice to interact with the mechanics and harmonics of the trumpet. Due to the nature of the harmonic series, the trumpet will, in some cases, force your voice to sing a specific pitch, and in others, change the timbre of the pitch that you are singing.

FIG. 2.1. Singing through the Instrument

You can also sing through the instrument while fingering different notes.

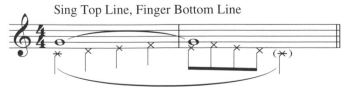

FIG. 2.2. Singing through the Instrument while Fingering Notes

There are a few methods of singing through the instrument, and each produces a slightly different sound:

1. Place the instrument on your face, and sing through your embouchure without buzzing.

2. Seal your lips over top of the mouthpiece, and sing.

3. Remove the mouthpiece, seal your lips over the mouthpiece receiver, and sing.

We'll look at singing and playing at the same time in lesson 20.

Exercises

Using each of the previous techniques, try the following exercises.

1. Sing a glissando from as low to as high as you can, in all valve combinations. Notice how this feels and what pitches result.

FIG. 2.3. Singing through the Instrument Exercise 1

2. Sing a steady pitch while moving your valves.

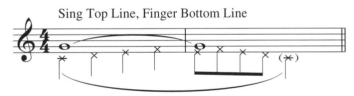

FIG. 2.4. Singing through the Instrument Exercise 2

3. Sing a steady pitch with different vowel shapes: AH, AY, EE, OH, and OOH.

FIG. 2.5. Singing through the Instrument Exercise 3

4. Combine any or all of the above.

3. MOUTHPIECE ALONE

Alternative Names: buzzing, mouthpiece buzzing, mouthpiece alone, mpc. alone

Sometimes, buzzing on only the mouthpiece can be very musical and yield interesting results. Buzzing on the mouthpiece has the added benefit of improving your conventional trumpet technique; the more you can control buzzing the mouthpiece alone, the more command you will have playing the trumpet. Furthermore, the more accurately you can buzz a melody, the easier it will be to play on the trumpet.

3

FIG. 3.1. Mouthpiece Alone Notation

An interesting mouthpiece-alone technique is to cup the shank of the mouthpiece between your hands to create a hand-trumpet. Buzz into the mouthpiece while opening and closing some of your fingers to create a *wah-wah* effect. The sound will change depending on how many and which fingers you use.

It's also possible to buzz your mouthpiece into mutes, jars, glasses, and just about anything else you can get your hands on to create different sounds.

4. VALVE AND SLIDE CLICKS

Alternative Names: valve clicks, slide clicks, percussive effects

One way to make percussion sounds on the trumpet is to click your valves and slides. Valve and slide clicks are a simple way to add percussion to any melody you are playing.

4

FIG. 4.1. Valve and Slide Clicks Notation

Exercises

1. **Valve Clicks**. Loosen your valve 1 cap slightly, and play a scale. You will notice when you play, that the upstroke of the valves make a snapping noise. To control this sound, you must take care to lift your finger off the valves at the precise moment you want to hear the sound. Repeat the process with cap 2 or cap 3 loosened instead of the first. The accents indicate where the valve cap will snap.

Valve 1 Cap Loosened

FIG. 4.2. Valve Clicks Exercise

2. **Slide Clicks**. Slide clicks can be made with the valve 1 and valve 3 slides. Depress the valve 3, and move the slide in and out against the valve casing. With some practice, you can gain control over the rhythm. For trumpets with a movable valve 1 slide, repeat the same process with valve 1.

Slide 3 Click

FIG. 4.3. Slide Clicks Exercise

Make sure that your valves and slides are always well oiled. Otherwise, techniques like this won't work well and could damage your instrument.

5. BELL PERCUSSION

Alternative Names: percussion, bell tapping

Bell percussion is when you tap an object on the bell of the trumpet. To start, use your fingernails or a pencil, since they are unlikely to damage your trumpet. If you are using your fingernails, try tapping against the inside of the bell. If you are using pen or pencil, try tapping against the rim of the bell. Experiment with tapping in different places to hear how it affects the sound.

5

Tap Bell

FIG. 5.1. Bell Percussion Notation

Remember that whatever you do, tap gently. It's very easy to dent or ding the bell of your trumpet if you strike it too hard.

Exercises

1. Tap a simple rhythm on your bell:

Tap Bell with Pencil

FIG. 5.2. Bell Percussion Exercise 1

2. Play a scale in half notes while tapping the same rhythm.

Tap Bell

Play

FIG. 5.3. Bell Percussion Exercise 2

6. MOUTHPIECE POPPING

Alternative Names: mouthpiece popping, popping, mouthpiece percussion

6

Mouthpiece popping is an easy way to add percussion to your playing. Mouthpiece popping is when you hit the end of your mouthpiece with the palm of your hand. This can be done with the mouthpiece alone or with the mouthpiece in the trumpet.

Mouthpiece Pop

FIG. 6.1. Mouthpiece Pop Notation 1

You will find that depressing the valves will change the tone and pitch of the pop. The pitch of the pop will be between low C and F♯, depending on the fingering. For example:

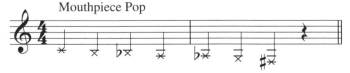

Mouthpiece Pop

FIG. 6.2. Mouthpiece Popping with Fingered Valves

The main challenge with mouthpiece popping is that if you strike too hard or accidentally twist the mouthpiece, you can get the mouthpiece stuck in the trumpet. So, at first, try popping the mouthpiece gently. Once you are comfortable that your mouthpiece won't get stuck, try playing different rhythms and change which valves are depressed.

If your mouthpiece does get stuck, contact a trumpet repair technician, or use a mouthpiece remover tool. Never use pliers, as you risk damaging both your trumpet and mouthpiece!

Exercise

Pop your mouthpiece rhythmically with a variety of fingering combinations and accents.

FIG. 6.3. Mouthpiece Popping Exercise

7. REMOVING SLIDES

Alternative Names: prepared trumpet, echo trumpet

A simple way to change your trumpet sound is to play with one of the slides removed. There are four slides that can be removed: The main tuning slide, and the valve 1, valve 2, and valve 3 slides. When a slide is removed, some notes will sound normally (such as the G and F-natural in figure 7.1), but some will sound different, such as the F-sharp.

FIG. 7.1. Removing Slides Notation

The pitch coming out the valve slide is often unpredictable and varies from instrument to instrument. In figure 7.1, on my own instrument, the sounding pitch is close to an A♭. In the examples on the next page and in the etude "Echo Echo," we have endeavored to demonstrate a few of the possible pitches. Experiment to see how it works on your particular trumpet, and if possible, keep a log of your results.

When you remove the main tuning slide and play, you will find that air no longer goes through most of the trumpet. This technique creates an amplified buzzing sound that is difficult to control. Although this technique is quite limited, it is worth exploring the sounds it can generate.

By removing a valve slide, the sound comes out the valve-slide pipe instead of the bell when that valve is depressed. This can create an interesting call-and-response effect when used with notes to which the valve doesn't relate.

Rather than removing all the valve slides at once, try to remove one at a time, and hear what happens.

Exercises

1. Remove the valve 2 slide on your trumpet, and hold a long middle G.

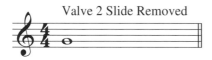

FIG. 7.2. Removing Slides Exercise 1

2. Alternate between middle G and F♯. Notice how when you play the F♯ (fingered second valve), the sound comes out where the valve 2 slide was.

FIG. 7.3. Removing Slides Exercise 2

3. Experiment with alternating between different fingering combinations to get familiar with how this technique works. For example:

FIG. 7.4. Removing Slides Exercise 3

8. SLAP TONGUE

Alternative Names: tonguing through your teeth

8

Slap tongue is a technique where you tongue between your lips without buzzing. This creates a "thupping" sound through the instrument. It is possible to do this rhythmically at a variety of speeds, or in uncontrolled rapid-fire succession.

FIG. 8.1. Slap Tongue Notation

As with mouthpiece popping, slap tonguing only produces a limited set of usable pitches.

FIG. 8.2. Pitches Produced by Slap Tongue

Exercises

1. Without the instrument, blow a steady stream of air. Push your tongue forwards until it touches the back of your top lip. This will block the air. Experiment with different speeds and volumes of air. Try doing it rapidly.

2. Repeat the process with the trumpet on your lips. Blocking the air with your tongue will cause the instrument to produce a faint pitch. Press down different valves to hear the different pitches.

3. Use this technique rhythmically, with a variety of valve combinations:

FIG. 8.3. Slap Tongue Exercise 1

4. Use this technique in a rapid-fire manner with a single valve combination.

FIG. 8.4. Slap Tongue Exercise 2

9. REMOVING VALVES

Alternative Names: prepared trumpet, echo trumpet

Another way to change the sound of your trumpet is to play with one of the valves removed. You will find that this technique mutes the sound of the trumpet. Like when removing your slide, the resulting pitch can be unpredictable, and vary from instrument to instrument. Experiment to see how it works on your trumpet.

FIG. 9.1. Removing Valves Notation

Exercises

1. Remove the valve 2 and play a middle G, fingered open. You may find that with the valve removed, the resulting pitch is actually an A, or possibly a different note. For the sake of this exercise, pitches notated represent what conventional fingerings to play, and don't necessarily reflect the pitch that you hear.

FIG. 9.2. Removing Slides Exercise 1

2. Play a G, while alternating between depressing valves 1 and 3.

FIG. 9.3. Removing Slides Exercise 2

3. Hold a long G while moving your finger in and out of valve 2 casing to create a pitch-bend effect.

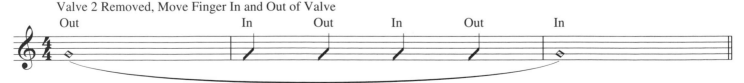

FIG. 9.4. Removing Slides Exercise 3

10. ALTERNATE FINGERING TRILLS

Alternative Names: valve tremolo, bisbigliando, color trill

10

Many notes on the trumpet can be played with more than one fingering. Rapidly alternating between different fingerings to play the same pitch produces a tremolo effect. Alternate fingerings may also be used to play rhythmically on a single note without the use of tonguing. Finally, this technique eases the difficulty of tricky passages or trills. You will find, however, that the pitch of alternate fingerings may vary slightly from the standard fingering, and thus may not always want to linger on them.

FIG. 10.1. Alternate Fingering Trills Notation. Numbers indicate fingerings.

Exercises

1. Play a middle G, fingered open.

FIG. 10.2. Alternate Fingering Trills Exercise 1

2. Next play the same pitch, but instead of fingering open, use valves 1 and 3.

FIG. 10.3. Alternate Fingering Trills Exercise 2

3. Hold the G steady and alternate between the open and the 1/3 fingering.

FIG. 10.4. Alternate Fingering Trills Exercise 3

Try alternating at different speeds and hear the timbre of the note change. Repeat this exercise on different pitches to gain control of it. Below is a chart of alternate fingerings up to high C. You will probably notice that as we play higher on the instrument, there are more alternate fingerings.

FIG. 10.5. Chart of Alternate Fingerings

11. VIBRATO

Vibrato is a standard technique employed by most trumpet players. Essentially, it is a small, controlled wavering of the pitch. Generally, you control vibrato by moving your jaw or right hand. Both types are acceptable and create different results. The pitch variation in your vibrato, however, need not be small. To create different effects, you can change the rate and size of the vibrato.

FIG. 11.1. Vibrato Notation

Exercises

1. **Jaw vibrato**. Hold a middle G. While holding the note, gently open and close your jaw a small amount. Notice how, when you open your jaw, the pitch drops, and when you close it, the pitch rises. Experiment with how far you can change the pitch.

FIG. 11.2. Vibrato Exercise 1

2. **Hand vibrato**. To begin, hold a middle G. While holding the note, gently rock your right hand back and forth on the valve caps. Notice how moving your hand away from you lowers the pitch while moving your hand towards you raises the pitch.

FIG. 11.3. Vibrato Exercise 2

3. **Learning to control your vibrato**. Put your metronome on quarter = 60, and hold a middle G. Try to pulse your vibrato to line up with every quarter note. Next, vibrate a bar or two of eighth notes, triplets, and sixteenth notes.

FIG. 11.4. Vibrato Exercise 3

12. HALF-VALVING

Alternative Names: ½ valve

12

Half-valving on the trumpet is a way to change the tone color and pitch as well as smear or slide around notes. The technique is relatively simple; instead of pressing the valve all the way down, press it part way and play a note. You will find that pressing the valve down to different depths produces different results. Generally, the closer to the fully depressed fingering you are, the more it will sound like the original note.

FIG. 12.1. Half-Valving Notation

Exercises

1. Play an F with valve 1. While playing, lift your finger a very small amount, and then press it down again. Notice the difference in timbre and pitch. Repeat this note while depressing the valve different amounts. You will find that when you lift the valve over halfway up, the pitch will change.

FIG. 12.2. Half-Valving Exercise 1

2. Play the same F with the valve semi-depressed. You may have noticed that in order to make a half-valve sound loud, you need to blow a little harder.

FIG. 12.3. Half-Valving Exercise 2

3. It's also typical to make a half-valve glissando up or down to a note. For instance, play a half-valved third-line B, and slowly raise your finger. You'll find this creates a small glissando effect between the B and the C. You can experiment to find on what other notes this works, and thus figure out how to do a descending glissando.

FIG. 12.4. Half-Valving Exercise 3

13. SLIDE BENDS

Alternative Names: glissando, microtones

13

Most intermediate and professional quality trumpets have movable valve 1 and 3 slides. This allows for a small measure of pitch control on notes that use these valves. The valve 1 slide can lower the pitch a little less than a quarter tone, while many valve 3 slides can lower the pitch as much as a semitone. In fact, the main purpose of slides 1 and 3 is to move certain notes on the instrument in tune. For instance, in order to play a low D in tune, you must move the slide 3 out around an inch.

FIG. 13.1. Slide Bend Notation

These slides can also be used to create bends and control microtones on certain notes. Unlike lip bends, using the slide to bend a note does not radically change the timbre of the note.

Remember, you can do a slide bend on any note that uses the first or third valve, including those with alternate fingerings! For instance, if you finger middle G with valve 1 and 3, you can use the valve 1 and 3 slides to lower and raise the pitch. The same can be done with any A, played with valve 3, and many other notes.

Exercises

1. Play a middle G.

FIG. 13.2. Slide Bend Exercise 1

2. Play the same note fingered valve 1 and 3.

FIG. 13.3. Slide Bend Exercise 2

3. While playing, move the valve 3 slide to see how it alters the pitch. Repeat the process with the first valve slide. Notice how you can't bend the pitch far with the valve 1 slide.

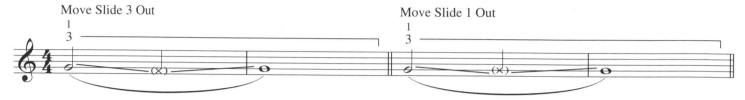

FIG. 13.4. Slide Bend Exercise 3

4. Alternate between the open fingering and the 1/3 fingering while moving slides 1 or 3. Make sure your slides are well oiled to get the most out of this technique.

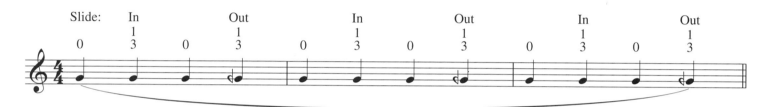

FIG. 13.5. Slide Bend Exercise 4. Note: the ⌀ accidental indicates a quarter tone.

14. FLUTTER TONGUING

Alternative Names: Flz, Flt, frull, or flutter may also be used in notation

14

Flutter tonguing creates a tremolo effect on the trumpet, and can be realized by rolling either the front or back of the tongue while playing a note. Both sound slightly different, so both can be mastered to achieve different results. Some players can't roll their R's both ways (or, in some cases, at all).

FIG. 14.1. Flutter Tonguing

Exercises

The method for practicing flutter tonguing with the front or back of the tongue is the same.

1. Try rolling continuously either the front or back of your tongue without the instrument. Try saying "TRRRRR" while rolling the "R."

2. Play a middle G while rolling your tongue. Try with both the front and the back of your tongue. You may find that in the beginning, you have to blow quite hard, and that it may seem forced. With practice, flutter tonguing is possible in even very soft dynamics.

FIG. 14.2. Flutter Tonguing a Whole Note

3. Play a slurred scale while flutter tonguing.

FIG. 14.3. Flutter Tonguing a Slurred Scale

4. If you are flutter tonguing with the back of your tongue, repeat the scale, only this time articulate each note:

FIG. 14.4. Flutter Tonguing with Articulations

15. GROWLING

15

Growling is a technique that was popularized by traditional jazz and big band-era trumpeters like Louis Armstrong, Cootie Williams, Bubber Miley, and Snooky Young. It is produced by making a guttural, growling hum in the back of your throat while playing. Because of the vocal element of the technique, it can make the trumpet sound like it is singing.

FIG. 15.1. Growling

Be careful not to overdo your practice of this technique. You can end up with a very sore throat or even seriously damage your vocal cords. Remember to rest as much as you play, and in the beginning, only practice this technique for a few minutes a day. Eventually, your endurance will build up, and you will have a clear sense how growling is affecting your throat.

Exercises

1. Away from the instrument, hum a low note. While humming, slowly tighten your throat until it starts to rumble and growl.

2. While "hum-growling," try to blow air out your mouth.

3. Bring the instrument up, and try to play a middle G while "hum-growling." You will probably have to be forceful at first to be able to play a note while growling.

FIG. 15.2. Growling Exercise

16. VALVE SECTION FLUTE

16

It is possible to blow across the hole in the bottom valve caps of the trumpet to create a flute-like sound. On my Yamaha trumpet, I am capable of sliding between F and A with this technique. The results vary from instrument to instrument.

FIG. 16.1. Valve Section Flute Notation

Exercises

1. Turn the trumpet upside down, and blow across the hole in one of the bottom valve caps.

FIG. 16.2. Valve Section Flute Exercise 1

2. Once you can achieve a steady tone, press the valve up and down for a slide whistle-like effect.

FIG. 16.3. Valve Section Flute Exercise 2

17. LIP BENDS

Alternative Names: bend, lip bend, note bend

17

A lip bend is when you deliberately lower a note without changing the fingering. These bends are a great way to add expression to your music and will add color to your sound. Many jazz players use lip bends to add inflection, and they are also used increasingly in microtonal contemporary classical music.

FIG. 17.1. Lip Bends

This technique is most easily learned in the middle-to-low register, but eventually, can be executed on the more difficult notes in the upper register, as well. Take your time, and be patient.

Exercises

1. Hold a middle G at a *mf* dynamic.

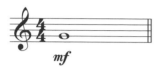

FIG. 17.2. Lip Bends Exercise 1

2. Without changing fingerings, force the pitch to bend down by slowly rolling your lips out and making a crescendo. Relax, decrescendo, and bring the pitch back up to the G. Repeat the exercise, but instead of making a crescendo, make a decrescendo.

FIG. 17.3. Lip Bends Exercise 2

FIG. 17.4. Lip Bends Exercise 3

3. Play the first five notes of a C major scale, with a lip bend on each note.

* numbers indicate fingers

FIG. 17.5. Lip Bends Exercise 4. Numbers indicate fingerings.

18. RIPS

Alternative Names: glissando, harmonic glissando

18

A rip is when you play rapidly from a very low note to a very high note while playing all the overtones in between.

Rip

FIG. 18.1. Rips

Exercises

Although these exercises indicate a two-octave rip, it is possible to rip up to any partial in the harmonic series.

1. Play a low C and slowly slur up to a G at the top of the staff or a high C, while playing all the partials in between.

FIG. 18.2. Rips Exercise 1

2. Repeat this process, but faster.

FIG. 18.3. Rips Exercise 2

3. Play as fast as possible.

Rip

FIG. 18.4. Rips Exercise 3

19. CIRCULAR BREATHING

Alternative Names: recurrent breathing, cycle breathing

19

Circular breathing is a technique that allows a player to continuously play notes without stopping for breath. Picture a bagpipe for a moment. Now replace the pipe with your trumpet and the bag with your cheeks. As you blow your horn, you fill up your cheeks with air. While squeezing the air from your cheeks, you breathe in quickly through your nose. During the whole process you never stop moving air through the instrument.

Circular Breathing

FIG. 19.1. Circular Breathing Notation

Before you learn to circular breathe on the trumpet, first practice the process away from the instrument.

Take a glass that is half full with water and a straw. Blow air through the straw to create a steady stream of bubbles. Inflate your cheeks, and switch from blowing air from your lungs to squeezing out the air in your cheeks. At that very moment, inhale as much air as you can through your nose, as quickly as possible, then immediately switch back to blowing air through the straw from your lungs. Repeat this process as many times as you can. The goal is to create a continuous stream of bubbles in the water.

Exercises

This exercise is adapted from John McNeil's *The Art of Jazz Trumpet* (Gerard & Sarzin Publishing Co., Brooklyn, New York).

1. With your mouthpiece alone, fill your cheeks with air, form an embouchure, and buzz by forcing air past your lips with your cheek muscles.

2. Repeat step (1), only this time, inhale through your nose during the brief time your lips are vibrating.

3. Repeat the drinking-straw exercise while buzzing to practice transferring support from the cheeks to the diaphragm, and back again.

4. Repeat steps (1) to (3) on the trumpet, this time trying to control the pitch. Start with a middle G.

It will take practice to get the timing down, but when you do, you should be able to sustain a note for long periods of time. It's normal at first for the pitch to waver, but with practice, you will be able to keep it more consistent.

20. SINGING AND PLAYING

Alternative Names: multiphonics, sung multiphonics, humming and playing

20

Singing and playing at the same time is a technique that allows you to play more than one pitch at a time on the trumpet. This technique is used primarily in contemporary classical and improvised music. On the trumpet, this works best when you play a low note and sing (or hum) a harmony note above it.

FIG. 20.1. Singing and Playing Notation

Exercises

1. Play a low C. Next, hum the same note strongly. Make sure you're singing it in the same octave, and not an octave below.

FIG. 20.2. Singing and Playing Exercise 1

2. Play a low E, and then hum it strongly, again making sure that you are singing in the right octave.

FIG. 20.3. Singing and Playing Exercise 2

3. Hum the E very strongly, then bring the instrument up to your face, and try to play a low C at the same time. If that doesn't work, try the opposite; first play the note, then sing above it.

FIG. 20.4. Singing and Playing Exercise 3

This might feel strange at first, but with a little practice, you can learn to control this technique and harmonize your own melodies. At first, singing a major third or perfect fifth above the note you're playing will be easiest.

Since this technique requires you to sing above the note you are playing, the higher you can sing, the more you can do with this technique. Normally, women find this technique easier than men because their singing voices are higher, and thus they have more control in the required range. Most men will have to sing at the high end of their range, usually in falsetto. Having said that, this technique can also be used in combination with pedal tones.

Although you can play sung multiphonics by singing below the notes, that tends to be less effective on the trumpet, and often results in a growl instead of harmony.

21. LIP SQUEEZES

21

To perform a lip squeeze, fill the space between your front teeth and lips with air, and squeeze out the pocket of air created without blowing. This often results in a high-pitched squealing sound. Lip squeezes can also be combined with circular breathing. For that, instead of filling your cheeks with air while you inhale, fill the area between your lips and teeth.

Lip Squeeze

FIG. 21.1. Lip Squeeze Notation

Exercises

1. With your lips alone, fill the space between your teeth and lips with air, and slowly squeeze it out. Experiment with different speeds of squeezing and lip tensions.

2. Repeat the process on your mouthpiece. This time, also see if you can control the pitch.

3. Finally, repeat the process on the trumpet. Experiment with how moving your valves and slides affect the sound.

22. SPLIT TONES

Alternative Names: multiphonics

22

As previously discussed, a multiphonic is when more than one pitch sounds at a time on the trumpet. Split-tone multiphonics are performed without singing into the instrument. Instead, two notes are produced with your embouchure. To begin, this is easiest between middle G and low C.

FIG. 22.1. Split Tones Notation

In the exercises, we will explore a couple of different methods for producing split-tone multiphonics. While this is a very challenging technique that requires a lot of patience, all things yield to practice.

Exercises

The first approach to split tones is achieved through lip bends.

1. Play a middle G, and bend it down with your lips down until it drops to low C.

FIG. 22.2. Split Tones Exercise 1

2. Play the G, bend down to the spot where the note dropped, and hold your embouchure there without dropping. From here, with some manipulation, you may hear two notes. With some practice and experimentation, you should hear, even if faintly, both a G and a C.

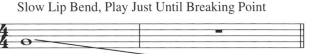

FIG. 22.3. Split Tones Exercise 2

The second approach to split tones involves playing while pushing your jaw out.

Play a low C and push your jaw out as far as you can. At some point, with some embouchure manipulation, the tone will begin to break up, and eventually your lips will vibrate more than one pitch.

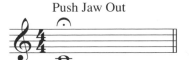

FIG. 22.4. Split Tones Exercise 3

Some people find that they can only play split-tone multiphonics softly, while others feel they have to start loudly. Experiment with which way works best for you.

23. EXTREME EMBOUCHURES

Alternative Names: fry, lip manipulation

23

It's possible to play sounds on the trumpet by taking everything we know about traditional tone production and disregarding it in favor of experimentation. Throughout the process of developing our good trumpet tone, we tend to focus on clarity, ease, pitch, and a number of other factors. This tends to result in a strong and flexible embouchure, an open air system, and a traditionally beautiful tone.

The development of extreme embouchures can result from efforts to play in nontraditional ways, which can seem forced, tense, or unnatural. This often produces unexpected sounds.

Before continuing, remember to rest as much as you play, always quit before you get tired, never play if it hurts, and abstain from negatively judging any sounds that come out of the instrument.

If you are not careful with these techniques you *will* injure your lips.

Below are some ideas for extreme embouchure experimentation:

1. Instead of using a regular trumpet embouchure, squeeze your lips together as hard as you can and blow, not worrying about what you hear. Experiment with different levels of lip tension and blowing.

2. Manipulate and squeeze your lips into different shapes, and play. Squish them off to one side, open them wide, or put them together in any way you can.

3. Change the shape of your oral cavity in extreme ways, from as open as possible, to as closed and tense as possible.

4. Push your jaw out or in to an extreme position. If you push your jaw out, try placing the mouthpiece firmly on the bottom lip and vice versa for pulling your jaw in.

5. Experiment with different levels of tension in your lips, oral cavity, tongue, throat, or air.

You may not recognize the sound coming out the bell as a traditionally trumpet sound. What is important is to experiment with different means of sound production, without negatively judging the result.

24. BOWING THE BELL

If you have a violin, cello, or bass bow, you can bow the bell of the trumpet. This technique creates a high-pitched ringing or scraping sound that is reminiscent of bowing a cymbal. Bowing the rim of the bell produces the clearest sound. You will find that the sound is slightly different depending on which direction and where on the bell you are bowing. Be careful with this technique, as it is possible to damage the lacquer or plating of the bell if you overdo it.

It is also possible to bow the bell while playing notes on the trumpet.

FIG. 24.1. Bowing the Bell Notation

Exercises

1. Bow the bell of your trumpet. The "∨" indicates an upstroke, and the "⊓" indicates a downstroke:

FIG. 24.2. Bowing the Bell Exercise 1

2. Play a C major scale in half notes, and bow the bell in whole notes:

FIG. 24.3. Bowing the Bell Exercise 2

25. MUTES

The basic principle of a mute is simple; you put something in or over the end of your bell to change the trumpet's sound.

FIG. 25.1. Mute Notation. Also: con sord./con sordino (*con* means "with"), senza sord/senza sordino (*sensa* means "without"). When using plunger or wah mutes: + (closed), o (open). Specific mute names are usually indicated.

There are many types of mutes that can change the sound of the trumpet. The most common types of mutes are straight, cup, wah-wah (Harmon), and plunger. Each type comes in a variety of models as offered by different companies. They come in a variety of materials (plastic, rubber, wood, metal, and even carbon fiber), and range from being relatively inexpensive to quite expensive. Each type and model of mute changes the sound of the trumpet in its own specific ways. Some mutes fit inside the bell of the trumpet, while others are held over the end. There are also a variety of less common mutes, including bucket, solo tone, buzz-wow, and pixie.

Keeping in mind the basic principle of what a mute is, you can experiment with making your own mutes, whether it's putting an aluminum pie plate over the bell, covering the bell with aluminum foil, playing into a jar or box, or even putting a kazoo into the bell. Experiment with various shapes and sizes of objects, as well as applying your mutes to different depths into the trumpet. Be careful to not put anything in too far and risk getting it stuck. Avoid plugging the trumpet entirely with your mute; you need to leave space for air and sound to escape.

Exercises

1. Find three household objects to make a mute out of. Try to find one flat object that will cover the bell, a second cylindrical object that will fit inside the bell, and a third flexible or cloth object that can be manipulated over or inside the bell.

2. Experiment with playing while moving each mute into different positions, and note the differences in sound. This can include varying degrees of covering the bell, depth of insertion, wah-wah motions, and beyond.

26. ELECTRONICS

One way to add a different dimension to your playing is to use electronic processing. This is especially important if you're playing electric jazz, certain types of avant-garde improvisation, or any type of popular music, which may require you to play at certain volumes and with sounds not readily available on the trumpet.

We recommend a basic setup that includes the following gear:

1. **Clip-on microphone + preamp**. Using a clip-on microphone gives you the freedom to move around a little bit on stage.

2. **Volume pedal**. We recommend a volume pedal for three important reasons. First, you always want to have an element of control over your volume on stage. If something accidentally feeds back or is much too loud on stage, you can adjust it instantly. Second, swelling with the volume pedal is an interesting technique when used in conjunction with other effects. Finally, some effect pedals, like an overdrive or distortion pedal, will increase the loudness of what comes out of the speaker, and can result in feedback without volume control.

3. **Reverb pedal**. It's likely that if you're performing live with a band, the guitar, vocals, and other instruments are going to have a certain amount of reverb and sustain. The trumpet does not naturally have this type of sustain, and using a reverb effect helps to blend with the other instruments.

4. **Digital delay pedal**. A delay pedal echoes what you play within certain parameters. This allows you to fill more space without playing more, and build short segments of looped material. Many delay pedals also have a looping function, which allows you to layer sounds.

5. **Powered speaker**. A 200-watt speaker is a good size to start with. You want to be able to play with enough volume without pushing your speaker's maximum loudness. Remember to face the speaker away from the microphone, as doing otherwise will result in feedback.

There are also a number of computer programs designed for live processing. Ableton Live, Apple's MainStage, Max/MSP, and Pure Data are leaders in the field, but there are many other programs available.

27. HOSE TRUMPET

It is possible to make your own valveless trumpet, or bugle, out of a hose and a funnel. Essentially, you attach a funnel to one end of a vinyl hose, insert your mouthpiece in the other, and play. You will find that the pitches that come out correspond to the harmonic series, much the same as playing all the pitches available in any single valve combination.

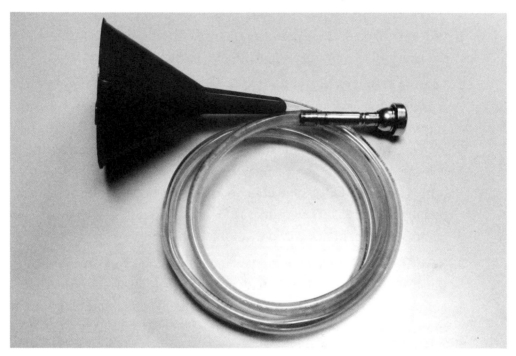

FIG. 27.1. Hose Trumpet

Materials:

- Five feet of hose or vinyl tubing with a 3/8" inner diameter

- A funnel that will fit over one end of the hose

- Duct tape or rubber cement

Assembly:

1. Attach the small end of the funnel to the hose. If the funnel does not stay on easily, duct tape or rubber cement it to the hose.

2. Insert mouthpiece. You'll notice that the 3/8" inner diameter allows for a secure fit.

3. Play!

The pitch of your hose trumpet will be flatter than your B♭ trumpet. On average, a B♭ trumpet measures 4 feet 10-1/4 inches long. Trim your hose trumpet to B♭ by cutting off a very short segment and checking the resultant pitch with your tuner. Continue this process until you reach the desired pitch. Be careful not to cut off too much at once.

PART II

Trumpet Sound Effects Etudes

The following etudes feature the sound effects described in part I. Each etude also has two audio tracks. The first is a full-band performance of each song, and the second is a play-along track.

1. BENDY BLUES

24
25

"Bendy Blues" uses two types of bends: the lip bend, and the slide 3 bend. It also uses alternate fingerings. The A section uses lips bends in a manner typical of jazz music, while the B section uses alternate fingerings and slide bends in a more contemporary manner.

BENDY BLUES

Craig Pedersen

2. POPPING PIECE

26
27

"Popping Piece" demonstrates using mouthpiece popping to create percussive grooves. Strike the cup of the mouthpiece firmly with the palm of your left hand, while using your right hand to play the fingerings for each indicated note. Make sure you move your valves and strike the mouthpiece at the same time.

POPPING PIECE

Craig Pedersen

3. WIND TUNNEL

28
29

"Wind Tunnel" alternates between using wind sounds, slap tongue, and conventional trumpet sounds to create rhythmic and melodic counterpoint. The square noteheads indicate wind sounds, while the x noteheads indicate slap tonguing. For these techniques, use the conventional fingerings indicated by the notated pitch.

WIND TUNNEL

Craig Pedersen

4. GET A RIP!

30
31

"Get a Rip!" uses two techniques: growling and ripping. These two techniques, which are often aggressive, are presented here in a more delicate manner. Both growling and ripping require you to move your air strongly, and to blow through each note. You may find that making a crescendo to the top of each rip makes playing the rip much easier.

GET A RIP!

Craig Pedersen

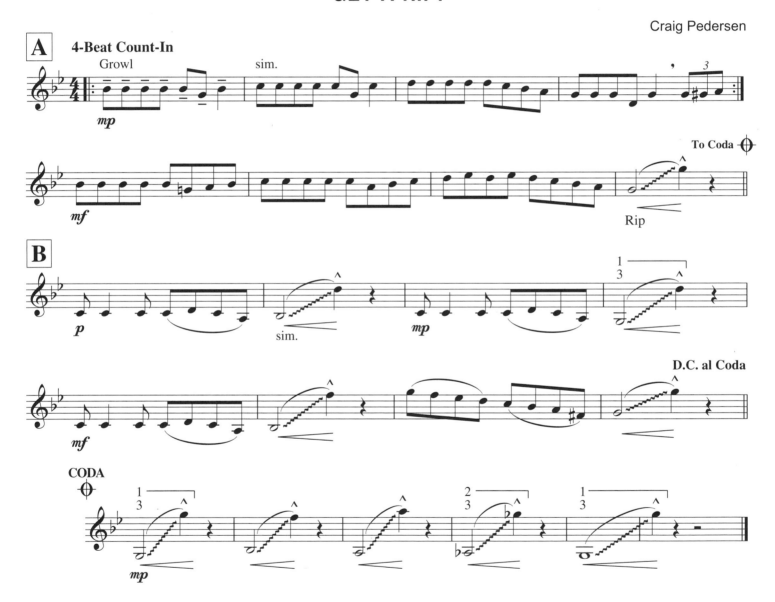

5. TAP IT

32
33

"Tap It" is an exercise in multitasking. While the trumpet melody is relatively simple, it is complicated by simultaneously tapping the bell with a pencil and by the 7/8 meter. Practice and master the parts independently before trying to put them together.

TAP IT

Craig Pedersen

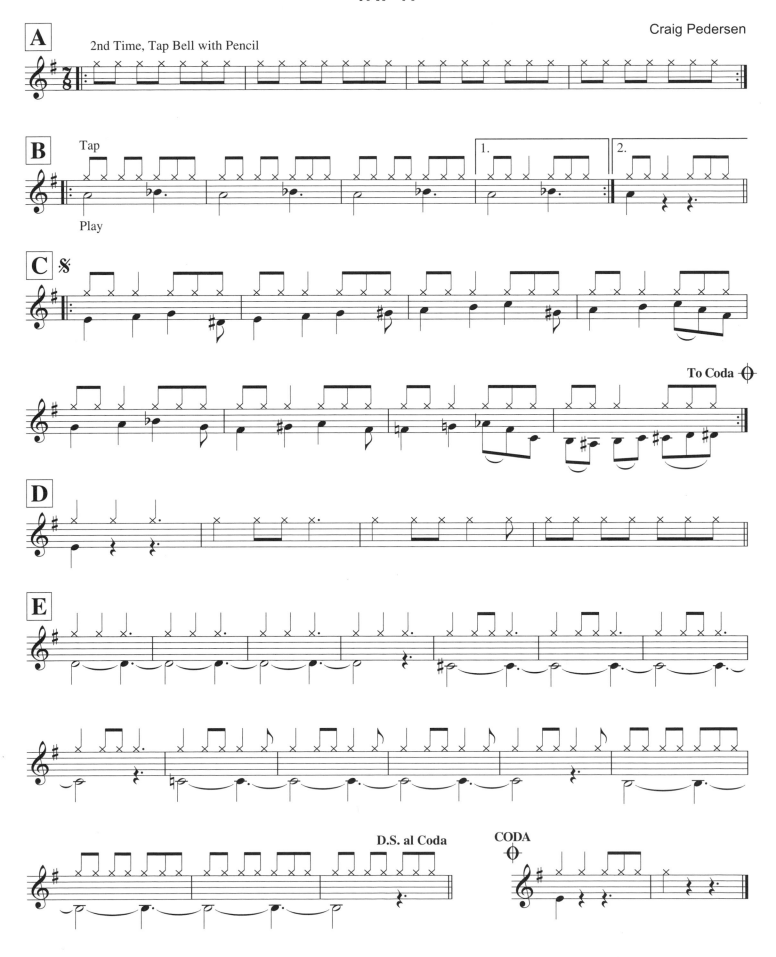

6. HALF SONG

34
35

"Half Song" uses half-valving in a manner typical of jazz music. Note the half-valve glissandi at the end of the B and the C section. These are played by slowly lifting the half-valve up until the pitch changes to the next note.

HALF SONG

Craig Pedersen

7. ECHO ECHO

36
37

"Echo Echo" uses the removal of the second valve slide to create an echo effect. As the pitches coming out of the valve-slide are often unpredictable, notes written indicate fingerings and the smaller noteheads above indicate an approximation of the resultant pitch.

ECHO ECHO

Craig Pedersen

8. FLUTTER CLACKER

38
39

"Flutter Clacker" uses both valve-cap percussion and flutter tonguing. Move your valves quickly on the upstroke for rhythmic precision, and blow strongly on the flutter-tongued notes. Use either front or back of mouth flutter tonguing.

FLUTTER CLACKER

Craig Pedersen

9. ALTERNATE REALITY

40
41

"Alternate Reality" uses alternate fingering trills, or valve tremolo, to create a rhythmic effect on sustained pitches. Remember to blow through each note as if you were sustaining the note without changing fingerings. The numbers above each note indicate fingerings to be used.

ALTERNATE REALITY

Craig Pedersen

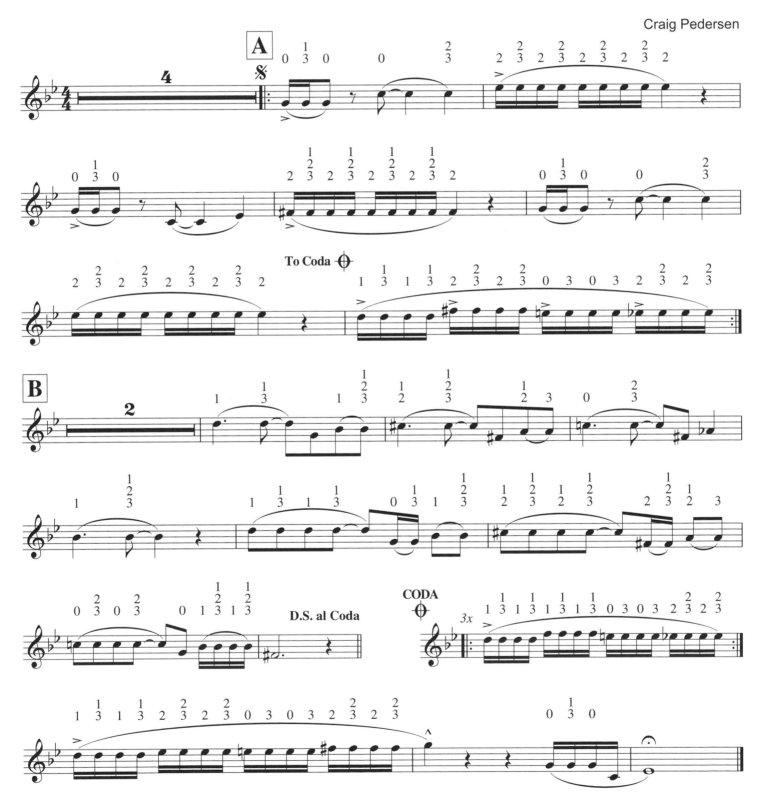

10. CIRCLES

42
43

The etude "Circles" is built around circular breathing. It is possible to play this whole study without *stopping* the airflow. Instead, circular breathe where breath marks are indicated.

CIRCLES

Resources

RECOMMENDED READING

Below is a list of books that have really influenced my approach in artistic use of extended techniques on the trumpet:

Bailey, Derek. *Improvisation: Its Nature and Practice in Music.* New York: Da Capo, 1993.

Blake, Ran. *Primacy of the Ear: Listening, Memory and Development of Musical Style.* Brookline, MA: Third Stream Associates, 2010.

Cassone, Gabriele. *The Trumpet Book.* Varese: Zecchini Editore, 2009.

Hickman, David, and Amanda Pepping. *Trumpet Pedagogy: A Compendium of Modern Teaching Techniques.* Chandler, AZ: Hickman Music Editions, 2006.

McNeil, John. *The Art of Jazz Trumpet.* Brooklyn, NY: Gerard & Sarzin, 1999.

Morris, Joe. *Perpetual Frontier: The Properties of Free Music.* Stony Creek, CT: Riti, 2012.

Schafer, R. Murray. *Creative Music Education.* New York: Schirmer, 1976.

Tolstoy, Leo. *What Is Art?* London: Penguin, 1995.

Vella, Richard, and Andy Arthurs. *Sounds in Space, Sounds in Time: Projects in Listening, Improvising and Composing.* London: Boosey & Hawkes Music, 2003.

Werner, Kenny. *Effortless Mastery.* New Albany, IN: Jamey Aebersold Jazz, 1996.

RECOMMENDED ARTISTS

There are many trumpet players in the jazz and classical community that are truly champions of using extended techniques with artistry. From a jazz and improvised music standpoint, we highly recommend looking into the music of Lester Bowie, Bill Dixon, Lina Allemano, Axel Dörner, Wadada Leo Smith, Rajesh Mehta, Franz Hautzinger, Don Cherry, Ingrid Jensen, Taylor Ho Bynum, Nicole Rampersaud, Peter Evans, and Nate Wooley. Each of these artists has developed a distinct personal vocabulary of musical expression on the trumpet.

From the standpoint of contemporary classical music, Håkan Hardenberger, Marco Blauww, Gabriele Cassone, Stephen Burns, Markus Stockhausen, Brian McWhorter, Amy Horvey, and Edward Carroll have shown themselves to be champions in the evolution of extended techniques on the trumpet, thanks in part to their close work with both composers and educating younger generations of trumpet players.

About the Authors

Craig Pedersen

Photo by David Barbour

Craig Pedersen is a trumpet playing performer/composer and educator based out of Montréal. He is an active freelance musician specializing in jazz and free music, also performing commercial and classical music. He actively leads his own band, the Craig Pedersen Quartet, and cofounded the Improvising Musicians of Ottawa/Outaouais concert series, a twice-a-month improvised music concert series in Ottawa, Ontario.

His activities as an educator are varied, from private lessons, teaching music in the public school system, coordinating and teaching at workshops, to curriculum design. His ongoing pursuits in music, study of instrumental pedagogy, organizational skills, and friendly, caring demeanor, help him to be flexible to the needs of all students, from beginners to advanced, at any age.

Visit him online at www.craigpedersen.com, where you can view his discography, musings on music, or contact him for a lesson. He teaches via Skype and iChat video.

Ueli Dörig

Photo by Martin Cavé

Ueli Dörig is a multi-instrumentalist, music educator, and performing artist. He grew up in Rorschach, Switzerland where he got a bachelor degree in education. After some years of teaching in public school and serving as a Swiss Army musician, he went on to study at Berklee College of Music in Boston, where he graduated with distinction in both performance and jazz composition. Since 2007, Ueli has lived in Canada's capitol region (Ottawa/Gatineau).

Other music books by Ueli Dörig:

• *Saxophone Sound Effects* (Berklee Press 2012)

• *Flute Sound Effects* (Berklee Press 2015)

• *Scale & Chord Studies for the Saxophone* (Royal Music Press)

Ueli Dörig on the Web:

• www.UeliDoerig.com

• www.ExtendedTechnique.com